ANN ARBOR DISTRICT LIBRARY

31621210227209

W9-ALM-228

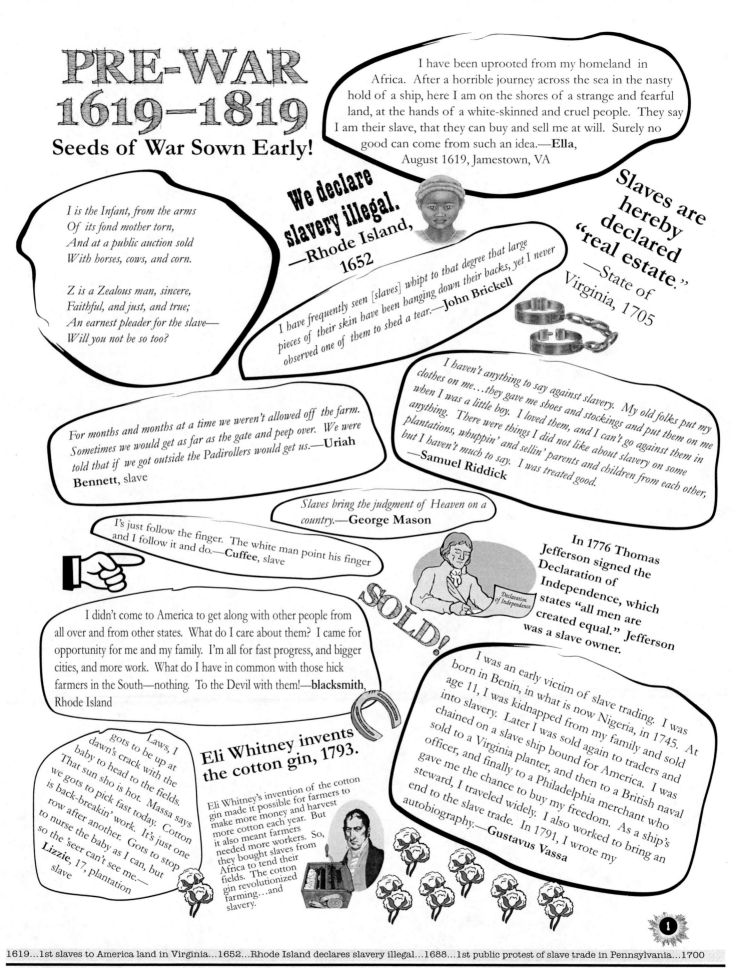

1619…1st slaves to America land in Virginia…1652…Rhode Island declares slavery illegal…1688…1st public protest of slave trade in Pennsylvania…1700

1829…A free black, David Walker, publishes an essay which encourages slaves to revolt. As a result, most southern states make it illegal to teach slaves to read and write…1830…Anti-Slavery Movement begins…1831…Maria Stewart is the first

The Fugitive Slave Act of 1793 demands the return of runaway slaves.

1820–1860 Antebellum="Before the War"

I don't know why some people can't understand the unity of the South. We have our own identity and traditions. Cotton is my crop and I need my slaves to make a successful living. If those darn Yankees came down here they'd see it's a lot of hot, hard hand-labor, no machine to magically get our crop in and meet the worldwide demand for cotton. Cotton is King, after all!—**plantation owner**, South Carolina

Antislavery newspapers began in 1821 with white editor Benjamin Lundy's *Genius of Universal Emancipation*. It had six subscribers.

COTTON IS KING!

abolitionist: person who worked to do away with slavery

Some people say "The South was built on the backs of blacks."

Slavery is a covenant with death and an agreement with hell.—abolitionist **William Lloyd Garrison**, *The Liberator*, Boston

It's like this: they's good massas and bad massas. Most white folks not slaves, but be about as po' as we slaves are! My plantation family's good to me.—**slave cook**, Louisiana

Slavery was sometimes called a "necessary evil" or the "peculiar institution."

Reveille is a bugle call that was used to wake up sleeping soldiers at sunrise. During the Civil War, the call was sounded between 4:45-6:00 in the morning! When the last note played, the flag was raised, a gunshot was fired, and the soldiers had to be dressed and ready for roll call.

A plot that involved 9,000 blacks, led by free black Denmark Vesey, was exposed in Charleston, South Carolina in 1822. Vesey and 36 others were executed.

I can't believe a man like that can be President of these United States! Andrew Jackson is nothing but a common man. Newspapers call him a "barbarian," "half-wit," and "tyrant," and I must say, I agree with them. The people got what they wanted, I guess…a low-class man running this whole nation!—**U.S. citizen**, 1828

Only one of every 20 Northerners was an active abolitionist.

I didn't have to be told that if a slave struck his master it meant death. Freeborn in North Carolina, but the son of a slave father, I knew slavery firsthand. My hatred of slavery drove me to Boston, where I sold old clothes and subscriptions to the *Freedom's Journal*. I burned to deliver my own message and in 1829 published my pamphlet, *Walker's Appeal.*—**David Walker**

For Sale

In 1831, slave Nat Turner led 70 blacks in a revolt that slaughtered 57 men, women, and children in rural Southampton County, Virginia. Troops rushed in to put down the uprising and killed over one hundred blacks—the innocent as well as the insurrectionists—in a savage massacre. Wild rumors and alarms swept through the South—could this happen again?!—**newspaperman**, North Carolina

I didn't know I was a slave until I found out I couldn't do the things I wanted.—Edmund, Georgia

I bet that was a shock!

…Virginia declares slaves are "property"…New York puts runaway slaves to death…1725 …Virginia grants slaves right to form own church…1739…Slave

black woman to lecture against slavery…William Lloyd Garrison publishes the first edition of the newspaper, Liberator, which called for emancipation of slaves…Nat Turner leads a slave rebellion in Southampton, Virginia…1833…The American and

THE STUDENT'S CIVIL WAR

150TH ANNIVERSARY EDITION • 1861-1865

CIVIL WAR RESOURCE BOOK

by Carole Marsh

Great balls of fire!

Battles, Battlefie...
Diagrams of a Fort, Uniforms,
Insignia, How to Make Hardtack,

Boo! Boo!

*Southerners were polite in calling slavery a "necessary evil." I call slavery a "positive good." I stand by what I said in Congress—slavery is good for blacks!—***John C. Calhoun**, South Carolina senator, 1837

*I was born a slave. I worked long and hard for my master 22 years. I finally ran away, and been hiding in a small space in my grandmother's attic for seven years. I'm trying to get to the North and gain my freedom. I finally have my chance. A boat is going to take me there tonight. Perhaps by morning, I'll be free!—***Harriet Jacobs**, North Carolina

How Come?

When I was born I was black.
When I grew up I was black.
When I'm sick I'm black.
When I go out into the sun I'm black.
When I die I'll be black.

But you:
When you were born you were pink.
When you grow up you are white.
When you get sick you are green.
When you go out in the sun you are red.
When you go out in the cold you are blue.
When you die you turn purple.
And you call me colored?

sesquicentennial: (noun) [ses-kwi-sen-ten-ee-uhl] a 150th anniversary or its celebration

$50 Reward!

Ranaway from the Subscriber, living in the county of Edgecombe, NC, about eight miles north of Tarborough, on the 24th of August last, a negro fellow named Washington, about 24 years of age, 5 feet and 8 or 10 inches high, dark complexion, stout built, and an excellent field hand, no particular marks about him recollected.

Maybe he's on the railroad?

Runaways Held in the New Bern, NC, Jail

Two New Negro Men, the one named Joe, about 45 years of age...much wrinkled in the face, and speaks bad English. The other is a young fellow...speaks better English than Joe, whom he says is his father, has a large scar on the fleshy part of his left arm.... They have nothing with them but an old Negro cloth jacket and an old blue sailor's jacket without sleeves. Also...a Negro named Jack, about 23 years of age...of a thin visage, bleareyed...has six rings of his country marks around his neck, his ears are full of holes.

I was born on a plantation near Fayetteville, North Carolina, and I belonged to J.B. Smith. He owned about 30 slaves. When a slave was no good, he was put on the auction block in Fayetteville and sold.
—**Sarah Louise Augustus**

What man can make, man can unmake.—
Frederick Douglass, abolitionist

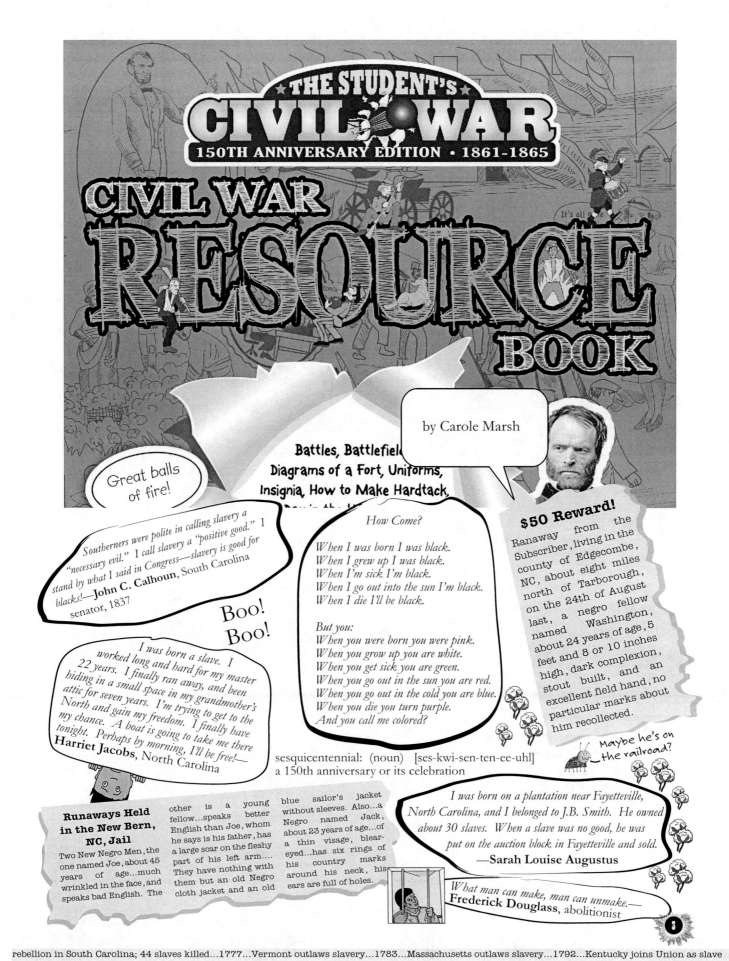

rebellion in South Carolina; 44 slaves killed...1777...Vermont outlaws slavery...1783...Massachusetts outlaws slavery...1792...Kentucky joins Union as slave

the Female Anti-Slavery Societies are formed in Philadelphia...1833...Oberlin College is the first coed college founded to educate African Americans...1837...The first Anti-Slavery Convention of American Women is held in New

Copyright Year of Our Lord 2010
Carole Marsh/Gallopade International/Peachtree City, GA

I thought it was the Year of the Tiger.

No, that was last year.

Oh.

Permission is hereby granted to the individual purchaser or classroom teacher to reproduce materials in this book for individual or classroom use only. Reproduction of these materials for an entire school or school system is strictly prohibited.

No part of this publication may be reproduced, stored in or introduced into a retrieval system, or transmitted, in any form or by any means (electronic, mechanical, photocopying, recording, or otherwise) without the prior written permission of the publisher of this book.

It takes an army to do a book. Here's ours:

HEADQUARTERS
Gen. Michele Yother, Gen. Mike Longmeyer, Master Sergeant Cowboy Pilot Bob Longmeyer
Indispensible Right Hand (Wo)man: Nancy "You Gotta Have" Hart

All you really need is heart, you know.

I know.

CIVIL WAR CENTRAL
Chief Wrangler: Paige Muh
Sergeant at Art Arms: John Hanson
Scribes, First Class: Whitney Akin, Janice Baker, Sherri Smith Brown
(Battle) Field Artists: Vicki DeJoy, Corie Ferguson, Yvonne Ford, Randolyn Friedlander, Jessica Talley
Erstwhile Intern: Emily Kimbell

John's relative walked home from the Civil War.

Oh, I thought he drove a Volkswagon.

That's the important people, right?

Absolutely.

GENERAL & ACCOUNTING
Muster Masters: Marcie Comeau, Cindy Green, Bri Roden

SALES
War bonds, right?   *Sure, wanna buy some?*   *Yeah, my old Confederate currency ok?*

Melessa Hill, Pam Morris, Gina Vranesevich, Lori White, Valerie Curry, Jennifer Johnson
Hallelujah Chorus: Denise Morris

MARKETING MILITIA
Head of the One-Million-Man E-mail March: Camille Chasteen
Linda Metoyer, Mark Dean, Tammy Weeks, Jennifer Kelly, Justin Badger

PRODUCTION & FULFILLMENT
Colonel James Barnard

I need fulfilling.   *You always do.*

Dave Guerrero, Pernell Arnold, Kathy Morgan, Jeff Jerabeck

SPECIAL UNIT
Hair and Makeup: Christina Yother
Dance and Funny Faces: Grant Yother
Cheerleader: Avery Longmeyer
PT, Boot Camp, and Gymastics: Ella Longmeyer
Best Boy: Evan "Da? Da?!" Longmeyer

I could use a makeover.   *Ya think?*

My kinda guy!

Cute legs!   *Whata sweetheart!*

I thought he was the key grip.   *That, too.*

Private First Class: CAROLE MARSH

Shouldn't she go up at the top?   *It's safer down here…out of the line of fire.*   *I'm just sayin…*

In 1849, there were 15 Northern and 15 Southern states. There were more people in the North, but since each state had 2 senators, there was a "stalemate" in the Senate at that time for any effort to pass laws.

I hate stale things!

*I remember all the bricklayers; they all was colored… The men that plastered the City Hall outside and put those columns up in the front…they was slaves, mos' all the fine work…was done by slaves. They called 'em artisans. None of 'em could read, but give 'em any plan an' they could foller it to the las' line.—*John H. Jackson

It took us as long as the war to get done!

Carole Marsh Civil War and Other Sassy Books for Young Readers are available from your favorite school supply or teacher store, almost all of America's fine museum and park stores, at lovely bookstores everywhere, or if all else fails, direct from www.gallopade.com, or call 1-800-536-2GET (that's 2438), extension 11, Miss Cindy.

We have referred to a few of our favorite Internet and social media sites throughout this book. All trademarks are registered, and belong to their respective owners—none of whom sponsored nor endorsed this book, nor are affiliated with Gallopade International/Carole Marsh Books.

For further information, trade terms, rights sales, good recipes, advice, and more, please contact:
GALLOPADE INTERNATIONAL
6000 Shakerag Hill
Suite 314
Peachtree City, Georgia
30269

You mean like when the wife stood on the hill and waved her hankie welcoming her Johnny home from the war?   *The very same!*

That's in the South, right?   *They made up that town name, right?*

Yes.   *Probably.*

See our bibliography and more at
www.studentscivilwar.com

I had to try to put an end to this political battle! When the territory of California applied to join the Union in 1849—as a free state—the U.S. had half free and half slave states. To stop this madness, I introduced a bill that would let California be a free state. However, my Compromise of 1850 also said that any new state could choose to be free or slave based on "popular sovereignty" or what the people wanted. After all, a state should have the right to decide what it wants to be, right? My bill passed, but alas, it was only a temporary solution.—Senator Henry Clay*, Kentucky*

4

…state…1793…The Fugitive Slave Act forces return of runaway slaves…Eli Whitney invents the cotton gin…1796…Tennessee joins Union as slave state…1800

…York…1839…Joseph Cinque leads a successful revolt on the slave ship, Amistad…1850…Congress passes the Fugitive Slave Act requiring captured runaway slaves to be returned to their owners. Whites now hunt slaves for profit…

A Word from the Author

There's a song that goes *"War! What's it all about? Absolutely nothing!"*

However war is usually about *something*. As you know, the Revolutionary War was all about America wrenching herself away from the final grasp of her mother country of England. It was a war to secure freedom, a new nation, and a new way of life. Later, no one looked back and said, "Hey, maybe we shouldn't have fought that war."

Close to a hundred years after America's founding, people were restless. America was now about a lot of ways of life, many quite different from the others. You might be a plantation owner using slave labor to grow your cotton crop. You might be a mountain woman still living in the wilds of Appalachia. You could be a president trying to run the still new, young, ambitious, and sometimes, even cantankerous and disagreeable country.

Two of the major disagreements of the mid-1800s were slavery and states' rights versus federal rights. Some folks said that they could not survive without slave labor, that they were good to their slaves, and that slavery was now a necessary and permanent part of American life. Others said slavery was wrong and that there was no reason any human being should be owned by another. After all, wasn't America about freedom for all people?

Some Americans thought that states should be able to make their own decisions without so much interference from the federal government in Washington. (Sound familiar?) Other Americans insisted that's what Washington and the federal government were for: to keep all states fair and equal and to solve disputes.

You could say that lanky, teenage America had major growing pains! But America was no longer a "kid." America was at a serious crossroads. Would Americans fight their fellow Americans over these issues? Could such disagreements be resolved by talking, cooperation, compromise, and change? Or would we go to war?

What a curious turn of events—to believe you had to fight your fellow countrymen to the death! Wasn't there any other way? As we know today, getting along and solving problems is much better than going to war. Sometimes, if you are under attack, you may feel you have no choice but to go to war to defend your nation, or to defend others.

Let's just say it was complicated. By the spring of 1861, Americans were actually talking about going to war. They made it sound necessary, even exciting. Many believed it would be a quick war—with their side winning, naturally!

Of course, it didn't happen that way. It was a long war—four years—with terrible tragedies. Slavery was ended. But not before most people "took sides" and fought face-to-face, often against people they knew or were related to, until no one any longer felt that war was a good thing, not even a so-called "necessary" war.

We're right!   NO!, we're right!

...Free blacks petition Congress to end slavery...Armed slaves rebel in Virginia; most are executed...1803...Ohio joins Union as free state...U.S. buys Louisiana

1853...Sarah Parker Remond is refused a seat in the Howard Athenaeum in New York. She takes the case to the police court, and the defendants are fined...1854...Frances Ellen Watkins Harper delivers her first anti-slavery lecture and publishes

What eventually led to war was a long, drawn out, complex, contradictory set of circumstances, actions, misunderstandings, and oversights. Could we have ended slavery and preserved the union—without war? Think about this, for it may be your job to assess, decide, act or not act, or argue for or against some similar situation one day!

As you read, imagine being that person at that time, in that place during that event. How would you feel, what would you do, how would you change? Today, could we possibly still "stumble" into such a long war? Would around-the-clock news make a difference? Would gathering those who disagree around a table and negotiating work? Diplomacy? The Civil War contains a world of wondering!

What was the American Civil War about? What did it mean? Was there another way? Was it fun, exciting? Was it fair? Who won? Who lost? What would you have done? What do you think?

Why does it matter what *you* think? Because in the absence of diplomacy, cooperation, collaboration, compromise, understanding, honor, and integrity, it is war, not peace, that always looms on our horizon. The past was in their hands. The future is in yours.

Carole Marsh
Shakerag Hill
Peachtree City, Georgia

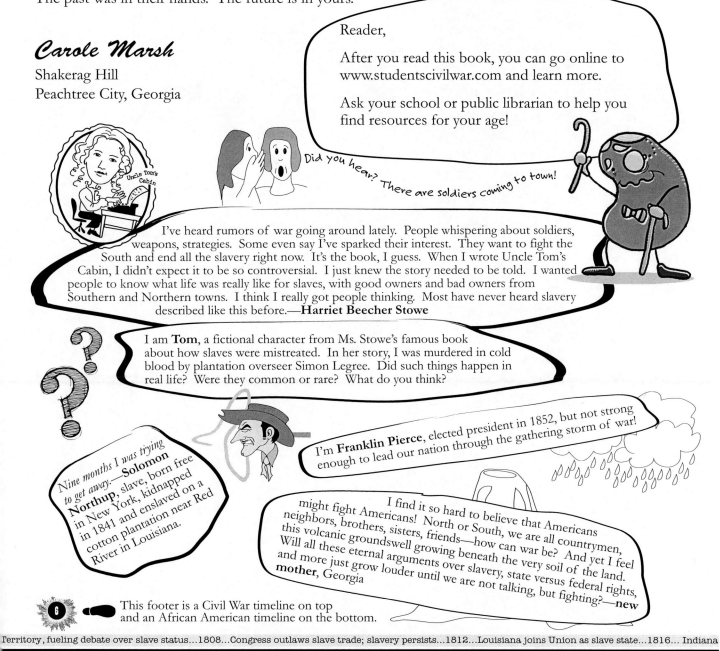

Reader,

After you read this book, you can go online to www.studentscivilwar.com and learn more.

Ask your school or public librarian to help you find resources for your age!

Did you hear? There are soldiers coming to town!

I've heard rumors of war going around lately. People whispering about soldiers, weapons, strategies. Some even say I've sparked their interest. They want to fight the South and end all the slavery right now. It's the book, I guess. When I wrote Uncle Tom's Cabin, I didn't expect it to be so controversial. I just knew the story needed to be told. I wanted people to know what life was really like for slaves, with good owners and bad owners from Southern and Northern towns. I think I really got people thinking. Most have never heard slavery described like this before.—**Harriet Beecher Stowe**

I am **Tom**, a fictional character from Ms. Stowe's famous book about how slaves were mistreated. In her story, I was murdered in cold blood by plantation overseer Simon Legree. Did such things happen in real life? Were they common or rare? What do you think?

Nine months I was trying to get away.—**Solomon Northup**, slave, born free in New York, kidnapped in 1841 and enslaved on a cotton plantation near Red River in Louisiana.

I'm **Franklin Pierce**, elected president in 1852, but not strong enough to lead our nation through the gathering storm of war!

I find it so hard to believe that Americans might fight Americans! North or South, we are all countrymen, neighbors, brothers, sisters, friends—how can war be? And yet I feel this volcanic groundswell growing beneath the very soil of the land. Will all these eternal arguments over slavery, state versus federal rights, and more just grow louder until we are not talking, but fighting?—**new mother**, Georgia

This footer is a Civil War timeline on top and an African American timeline on the bottom.

Territory, fueling debate over slave status...1808...Congress outlaws slave trade; slavery persists...1812...Louisiana joins Union as slave state...1816... Indiana

her first book of verse ...1857...With the Dred Scott Decision, the U.S. Supreme Court denies citizenship to black people...1859...White abolitionist, John Brown, leads a raid at Harper's Ferry. He is captured and sentenced to death...1861...Civil

Civil War Music

Much like today, music was very important and popular during the Civil War. Soldiers loved to sing, but they did not go on tour, play concerts, or win Grammys like today's artists! Music was used to send secret messages during battle and to announce daily activities from sunup to sundown. Happy songs were played to keep the soldier's spirits high during battle, while sad songs were sung when the soldiers were lonely and longed for home. Many times, if soldiers liked a tune they heard the enemy singing, they would write their own words and sing it themselves. That's why many Civil War songs have two sets of lyrics! When the soldiers weren't fighting, they would spend their evenings singing and writing songs. Men would sit by the campfire singing and playing along with guitars, banjos, drums, flutes, and harmonicas. Some soldiers even made their own instruments from string and wood boxes! "When Johnny Comes Marching Home," "Dixie," and "Here's Your Mule" were popular songs that both the Union army and Confederate army liked to sing.

BATTLE OF THE BANDS

Did you know the first Battle of the Bands happened during the Civil War? In the winter of 1862-1863, the Union army and Confederate army both camped at Fredericksburg, Virginia with only a river separating them. One cold afternoon, the Union band started playing upbeat tunes to cheer the soldiers. When the song ended, they heard the Confederate army playing the same song from across the river. For hours, the Union army would play a song and the Confederates would try to play it better. Finally, the duel ended when both bands began playing "Home, Sweet Home," and all the men started to cheer!

ACTIVITY

Make your own campfire instrument just like the Civil war soldiers.

Supplies needed:
Empty tissue box
String
Tape

Cut string into three or four long pieces. Tape the string pieces over the tissue box hole. Make sure the strings are tight. If you want to add a handle, tape or glue a paper towel roll onto the tissue box. Now you have your own campfire guitar! Play along while the soldiers sing "Dixie!"

Look away! Look away! Look away! Dixie Land.

*Lyrics and performances of Civil War songs can seen/heard at http://www.civilwarmusic.net/songs.php

joins Union as free state…1817…Mississippi joins Union as slave state…1818…Illinois joins Union as free state…1819…Alabama joins Union as slave state…

War begins…Charlotte Forten Grimke becomes a volunteer teacher of freed men on St. Helena Island in South Carolina…1863…Harriet Tubman leads a military raid on the Combahee River in South Carolina and helps hundreds of slaves escape

Civil War Money

The Confederate States of America began to issue its own currency only two months after its formation. Since none of the Southern states had gold or silver, money was backed by cotton. The Confederates believed that when they won the war, their money would gain worth. The pictures on their money were not of Abraham Lincoln or the White House. They had pictures of "President" Jefferson Davis, "Vice President" Alexander Stephens, General "Stonewall" Jackson, and of slaves. As the South began to lose the war, their money began to lose value. By the end of the war, a bar of soap cost $50! When the Confederacy surrendered, their money was completely worthless and could not buy anything. Rich plantation owners became poor overnight!

ACTIVITY

Make your own currency!

Draw your own paper bills. You can draw whatever you want on your money—even your dog! Make the bill worth anything from one dollar to 1,000 dollars!

VALUE CERTIFICATE

QUIZ

- Can Confederate money be used to buy something at the store today?
- How much is Confederate money actually worth today?

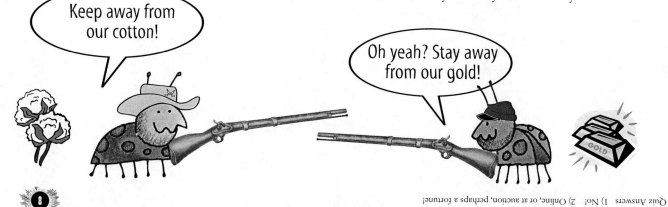

Keep away from our cotton!

Oh yeah? Stay away from our gold!

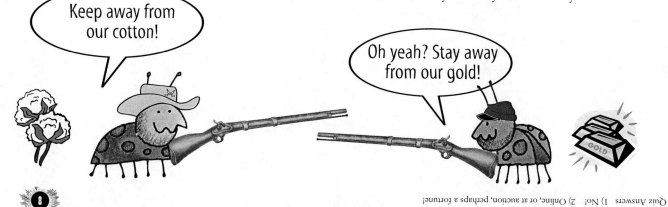

Quiz Answers 1) No! 2) Online, or at auction, perhaps a fortune!

New ▾ | Print | Delete | Day | Work Week | Week | Month | View Date | Categories ▾ | Projects ▾

5:00 AM	Reveille & Roll Call: Drums or bugles awakened soldiers out of small canvas "dog tents" to start a long, arduous day.
5:30 AM	Breakfast: Hardtack and coffee cooked over open campfire.
6:00 AM	Sick Call: Sick and ailing soldiers reported to surgeon's tent for medical attention and elixirs.
7:00 AM	Marching Drills: Squads and companies practiced formations to drumbeats and drum signals.
8:00 AM	Manual of Arms: Soldiers cleaned, primed, and practiced loading muskets and rifles.
9:00 AM	Camp Upkeep: Various jobs performed around camp such as digging latrines (yuck!), chopping wood, building log huts in the winter months, mending uniforms, rationing food.
11:00 AM	Free Time: Soldiers had long periods of boredom and leisure time in camps (ironically wedged between periods of fear and terror on the battlefield). Men passed the time playing cards, dice, baseball, writing letters home, reading, pitching horseshoes, cheering on lice races, and sleeping.
12:30 PM	Mail Call! A celebratory event for all soldiers! Men would read and re-read letters from home. The very lucky ones received care-packages from home filled with baked goods, toiletries, new socks or shirts. No member of camp was happy if the mail arrived to camp late!
1:00 PM	Battle: Short battles between small groups of soldiers could last only five or six hours. But most battles lasted at least one or two whole days!
6:00PM	Bury Dead: After battle, living soldiers had to bury the dead in order to prevent disease. Union soldiers were usually buried in trenches, while Confederate soldiers were usually buried in a mass grave.
7:00PM	Dinner: Soldiers were given food rations at the beginning of the week. For three days, this was all the food soldiers had to eat. They had to make it last. Men were given pork, rice, peas, beans, potatoes, and dried fruit.
8:00PM	Church Service: Many soldiers attended church service on a regular basis. Many regiments had a chaplain that would travel with the army. Chaplains would hold services for the soldiers, work in hospitals comforting the sick and wounded, and write letters home for those who could not write.
8:30PM	Campfire Singing: During the evenings soldiers loved to sit around the campfire and sing. They sang songs about battles, their country, and home.
9:00 PM	Guard Duty: One of the most dreaded duties assigned to soldiers. Why? Because of the fear of falling asleep while on duty! Falling asleep on guard duty or other such offenses drew serious punishment from commanding officers—such as beatings, "bucking and gagging," or performing embarrassing tasks.

Compromise blocks extension of slavery above latitudinal line of 36°30' north…1822…Slaves revolt in South Carolina; 37 are hanged…1827…New York

withdrawing federal troops from the South…1880…Post Reconstruction era begins…The policy of white supremacy in the South leaves black people segregated, disenfranchised (without opportunity), and oppressed…1895…First National

Bloodshed

No one knows exactly how many people were killed during the Civil War. Unlike today, no one took the time to keep a record. Historians estimate that 618,000 soldiers were killed! Sadly, over 66% of the men died of disease. Still, the Civil War is considered one of the bloodiest wars. Over 203,940 men died during battle from a gunshot or wound. But how much blood was actually shed?

Sad Civil War Math

• A man must lose 40% of his blood to have a life-threatening condition or death. If there are 5 liters of blood in an average adult, how many liters of blood must be lost before death occurs?

• If there are 33.5 ounces in one liter, how many ounces of blood must be lost before death?

• Wow! That means that one man that died during battle lost 4 pounds of blood! If 618,000 soldiers died, how many ounces is that total?

• This is where the math gets tricky! We want to know how many total gallons of blood were lost during the Civil War. If 128 ounces equal 1 gallon, then 13,663,980 ounces would equal how many gallons? We will have to round to get this answer! Round your answer to the nearest hundredth place.

• One last problem! We want to know how many tanker trucks of blood that is. If one tanker truck can hold 9,000 gallons, how many tanker trucks would it take to hold all that blood that was lost during the Civil War? We have to use rounding again for this problem! Round your answer to the nearest whole number (no decimal).

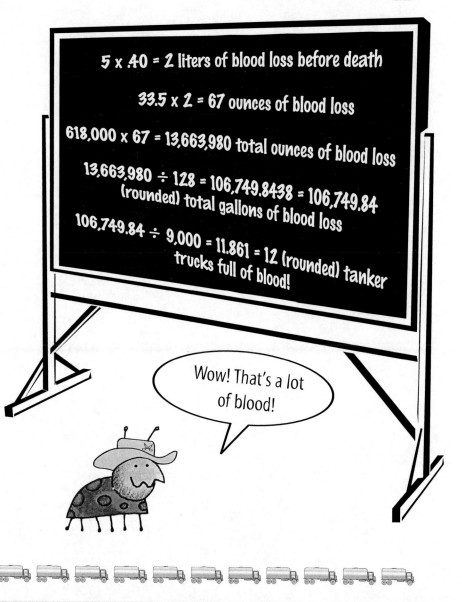

$5 \times .40 = 2$ liters of blood loss before death

$33.5 \times 2 = 67$ ounces of blood loss

$618,000 \times 67 = 13,663,980$ total ounces of blood loss

$13,663,980 \div 128 = 106,749.8438 = 106,749.84$ (rounded) total gallons of blood loss

$106,749.84 \div 9,000 = 11.861 = 12$ (rounded) tanker trucks full of blood!

Wow! That's a lot of blood!

...tlaws slavery...1828...South Carolina insists states can void federal laws...1830...Congress debates states' rights vs. federal government...1831...Abolitionist

nference of Colored Women is held in Boston...1896...The U.S. Supreme Court upholds segregation in its "separate but equal" doctrine set forth in the Plessy vs. Ferguson case...Mary Church Terrell graduates from the Women's Medical

A Civil War Sub

During the Civil War, President Lincoln used the U.S. Navy to blockade Southern ports. The strategy was to keep supplies from reaching Confederates. The South needed a way to break through the blockades. H.L. Hunley, a Southerner, began work on a submarine.

The *H.L. Hunley*

On February 17, 1864, the C.S.S. *Hunley* sank the U.S.S. *Housatonic*. The *Hunley* became the first submarine to sink another ship. The *Housatonic* sank in about three minutes. The *Hunley* crew signaled Confederates onshore with a blue light. Mysteriously, the *Hunley* sank immediately.

For many years, adventurers searched for the *Hunley* with no luck. Circus showman P.T. Barnum once offered $100,000 for anyone who found and recovered the sunken submarine. Finally in 1995, author Clive Cussler and his National Underwater Marine Agency discovered the submarine under 30 feet of water and about 3 feet of silt near the mouth of Charleston Harbor. On August 8, 2000, the *Hunley* was raised. Research on the *Hunley* continues at the Warren Lasch Conservation Center in Charleston, South Carolina.

Build a Pen Cap Submarine

Here's what you will need:
- *A pen cap*
- *Modeling clay*
- *A 2 liter plastic bottle (with cap)*

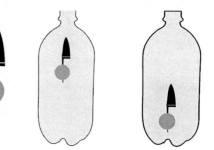

1. Put a ball of clay on the stem of the pen cap.
2. Pour the water into the plastic bottle until it is almost full. Put the pen cap ("submarine") in bottle with the top pointing up. Add or subtract until the "submarine" floats just below the surface of the water. It now has neutral buoyancy.
3. Completely fill the plastic bottle with water and put the bottle cap on tightly.
4. Squeeze the bottle. This will cause the pressure inside to go up and the air trapped inside the pen cap will shrink. This will change the buoyancy of your "submarine" from neutral to negative and it will sink to the bottom. When you release the pressure the air will expand and the sub will rise.

Hey this is fun!

William Lloyd Garrison publishes The Liberator...Slave rebellion in Virginia leads to tougher slave laws...1832...Congress passes new tariff law, benefiting

College of Pennsylvania...1909...The NAACP is founded...1920...The Nineteenth Amendment gives women the right to vote...1935...Federal Writers' Project established by Franklin Roosevelt...fieldworkers were assigned to travel through

It Was All About the Weapons!

Really, it took a "village" of weapons to duke it out in the Civil War. Let's take a look at some of the well-equipped soldier's tools of war.

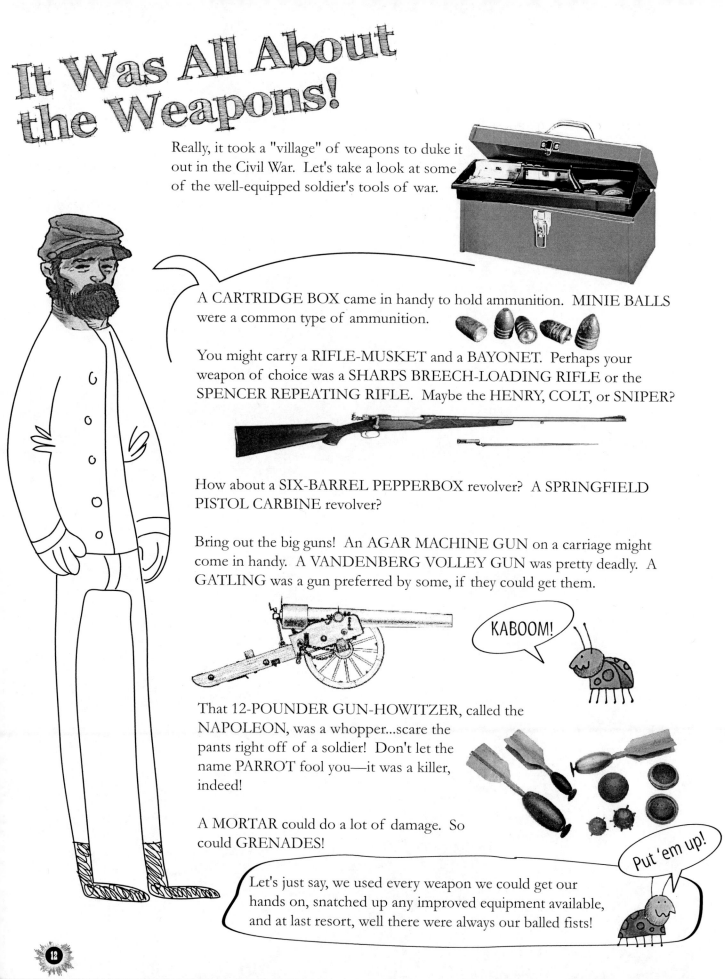

A CARTRIDGE BOX came in handy to hold ammunition. MINIE BALLS were a common type of ammunition.

You might carry a RIFLE-MUSKET and a BAYONET. Perhaps your weapon of choice was a SHARPS BREECH-LOADING RIFLE or the SPENCER REPEATING RIFLE. Maybe the HENRY, COLT, or SNIPER?

How about a SIX-BARREL PEPPERBOX revolver? A SPRINGFIELD PISTOL CARBINE revolver?

Bring out the big guns! An AGAR MACHINE GUN on a carriage might come in handy. A VANDENBERG VOLLEY GUN was pretty deadly. A GATLING was a gun preferred by some, if they could get them.

KABOOM!

That 12-POUNDER GUN-HOWITZER, called the NAPOLEON, was a whopper...scare the pants right off of a soldier! Don't let the name PARROT fool you—it was a killer, indeed!

A MORTAR could do a lot of damage. So could GRENADES!

Put 'em up!

Let's just say, we used every weapon we could get our hands on, snatched up any improved equipment available, and at last resort, well there were always our balled fists!

Northern industry...South Carolina nullifies federal edict, calls for secession...President Jackson declares no states may leave Union...1833...Lucretia Mott

outhern states to gather life histories of ex-slaves...1940...Ella Jo Baker, a dedicated organizer in the freedom movement, begins work in the South as field secretary of the NAACP...1941...Civil Rights Movement begins...Thousands of black

A is for Artillery

What would a war be without artillery and ammunition? The Civil War certainly had its share of artillery. Artillery was the "big guns," so to speak, versus small arms and weapons. Even the names of field artillery had "big gun" names:

Artillery required ammunition. Four types used in the Civil War included:

SOLID: an iron shell (ball) filled with powder and a fuse.

SHELL: a hollow projectile filled with 90% black powder; very explosive!

SHRAPNEL: a hollow shell (ball) filled with about 70 iron balls and a bursting charge.

CANISTER: a thin metal can filled with iron or lead balls in sawdust.

WHITWORTH   *12 POUNDER*

HOWITZER

NAPOLEON 12 POUNDER

Needless to say, all these were destructive and deadly. However, Civil War-era ammunition was often unreliable, with as high as a 50% failure rate.

And then there was the Parrot Cannon, 3-inch Ordnance rifle, and James Rifle (the last two still "cannons").

Ammunition and Artillery Trivia

 One cannon could shoot a shell as far as 3,000 yards!

 The powder used produced stinky, eye-irritating black clouds of smoke!

 Firing a cannon was hard work. After a cannon was fired (and so moved), it had to be quickly repositioned, usually being reloaded as it was moved!

 A crew could load, aim, and fire twice in one minute!

 The capture of field cannons was considered a highly-desired prize!

As an example, about 55,000 rounds of ammunition were fired at Gettysburg!

Ready!

Fire!

Aim!

13

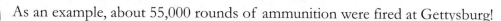

forms Female Anti-Slavery Society...Theodore Weld forms American Anti-Slavery Society...Ohio's Oberlin College 1st to admit blacks...1835... South Carolina

people organize to press their demands for justice... President Roosevelt issues an executive order against discrimination of workers in defense industries and government...1942... Margaret Walker wins the Yale Award for Young Poets for her

The Engineers

It took a lot of folks to fight the Civil War. Some were involved in strategy, others as thick-of-the-fight soldiers, some trailed behind to clean up the mess. But important to the war effort were the engineers. Here are just some of the useful things they built.

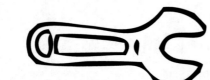

A CORDUROY ROAD

This kind of road was made by laying planks down sideways over long rows of logs. This let men and equipment move through muddy fields without getting bogged down.

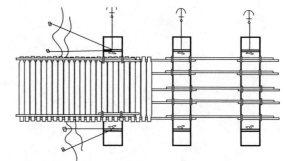

FORTS

We can easily picture the brick walls, moats, and other parts of forts that we can still visit today at various Civil War historic sites.

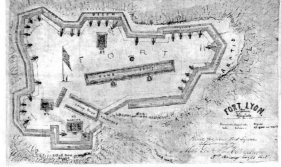

FORTIFICATIONS

Just as important were fortifications, often erected quickly, and of materials at hand. Some fortifications were temporary, others permanent.

BRIDGES

Engineers also built pontoon bridges across the many streams and rivers necessary to cross to get to the enemy.

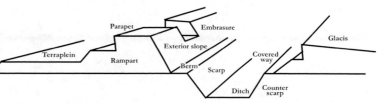

ourns abolitionist literature…Georgia threatens to enact death penalty for abolitionist writers…Abolitionist William Ellery Channing publishes Slavery…1836

moving collection of poems, "For My People"…1947…Lawyer and economist, Sadie T.M. Alexander is appointed to Truman's Commission on Civil Rights…CORE sends its first group of "Freedom Riders" through the South…1948… President

Civil War Codes

During war, it is very important for an army to have a secret code. If a message is sent in a secret code, the enemy won't be able to read it. During the Civil War, the North and South used a secret code called cryptography. Cryptography is when one letter of the alphabet stands for another letter of the alphabet. It can be very confusing! The men who deciphered the messages had a special tool called a cipher wheel that helped them break the code!

Cipher Wheel

Can you "Break the Code?"

This is a special message for Confederate President Jefferson Davis from the first general of the Confederate army. Looks like the Confederates are about to start the Civil War! Can you discover where the Confederates plan to attack first?

Some secret messages were even hidden in a false tooth!

I SPY

Women were very crafty at getting secret messages passed around.

Special Message for President Jefferson Davis

Alphabet Letter	A	B	C	D	E	F	G	H	I	J	K	L	M	N	O	P	Q	R	S	T	U	V	W	X	Y	Z
Code Letter	O	H	J	R	N	G	W	D	U	X	V	M	C	E	I	A	K	Z	F	B	S	L	Q	Y	E	P

B D N   J I P G N R N Z O B N   O Z C E   U F   Z N O R E

B I   O B B O J V   G I Z B   F S C B N Z   W N P N Z O M

H N O S Z N W O Z R

Let me get my cipher wheel!

Vtg rhn znxll patm B'f ltrbgz?
(Can you guess what I'm saying?)

If you want a different message use this link to make the puzzle-
http://puzzlemaker.discoveryeducation.com/cryptogramSetupForm.asp

Answer= THE CONFEDERATE ARMY IS READY TO ATTACK FORT SUMTER! –GENERAL BEAUREGARD

15

...Arkansas joins Union as slave state...1837...Michigan joins Union as free state...1845...Florida joins Union as slave state...Texas joins union as slave state

Truman issues an executive order banning segregation in the armed forces...Pharmacist Ella Nora Phillips Stewart is elected president of the National Association of Colored Women...Edith Irby Jones is the first black to be admitted to a Southern

Civil War Reenactments

The Civil War was a major part of American history and is still commemorated today. Many people honor the brave soldiers who fought during the war by hosting pretend battles called reenactments. Men dress up in old army uniforms, carry weapons, and head to the field for battle! These men study everything about the Civil War. They even train like a real Civil War soldier! For a whole weekend, these men pretend to be in war. There are reenactments held in California, Missouri, Texas, Ohio, Illinois, and all over the country. People come to watch these men perform the reenactment and remember all the courageous soldiers who fought during the real Civil War. Women also participate, as do children!

ATTACK!

CHARGE!

That looks like fun!

Have a Classroom Civil War Reenactment!

Bring the Civil War to life in your classroom by hosting a "reenactment" of a famous event in the war, or a battle or other event that took place in your area or state.

Have students work on costumes, props, and other materials to reflect everyday Civil War life, on and off the battlefield. Set up "scenes" by staging a few students together perhaps preparing hardtack, setting up a tent, writing letters back home, preparing for battle, etc. Either before or after, try to visit a real Civil War reenactment to get ideas. Also see the page in this Resource Book about building a classroom Civil War Cyclorama, and use that as your backdrop. Coordinate with another class to enlarge and enhance this project.

Check for local reenactment groups in your area that might let you borrow props or otherwise participate in your project, such as speaking to the class. Students can "role play" by memorizing certain things to say as the Civil War character they represent. Invite other students to visit the campsite or battlefield. Play Civil War era music or have students play a fife or drum. Serve Civil War era food. If possible, have background sound effects of distant cannon fire, for example.

Do all you can to bring it to life! Do the best you can and video it for reference to do again in the next school year!

16

..1848...Wisconsin joins Union as free state...Treaty of Guadalupe Hidalgo signed ending Mexican War—U.S. gains Texas, California, and all land in between...

medical school, The University of Arkansas...1954... In the Brown vs. Board of Education Case, the U.S. Supreme Court declares segregation in public schools unconstitutional...1955...The U.S. Supreme Court orders school integration "with all

Letters Back Home

During the Civil War many soldiers wrote letters back home to their parents, friends, wives, and children. Letters were the only way for a soldier to keep in contact with his loved ones. The Union Army had a post office near forts where soldiers could purchase stamps and send their letters. In 1864, the Union Army was allowed to send letters home for free as long as they wrote "Soldier's Letter" on the envelope.

Confederate soldiers had a difficult time sending letters. Stamps, papers, pens, and pencils became very scarce in the South. Confederate soldiers often stole stationery from Union prisoners so they could write home. Soldiers wrote of their battle and campground experiences and usually told their families not to worry. Luckily many letters survived the war, and can still be read today!

Activity: Write a Letter

Imagine you are a soldier during the Civil War and have the opportunity to write home to your family. What would you say? Write a letter back home telling friends and family about your experiences. Don't forget to write "Soldier's Letter" on the envelope, so you can send your letter for free!

Make Ink from Berries!

Not only did soldiers have to scrounge for paper, ink was often not to be had. Soldiers improvised and made ink from berries. When there were no quill pens to use, they wrote with cornstalks! Envelopes might be made from old letters. And some letters were written in between the lines of letters they received!

A letter from my sweetie!

You gonna eat that?

Berry Ink

Put 1/4 cup strawberries or raspberries in a bowl; crush them with the back of a spoon until a smooth liquid.

1850...Congress passes the Compromise of 1850...1852...Harriet Beecher Stowe publishes Uncle Tom's Cabin...1854...Congress passes the Kansas-Nebraska

deliberate speed."...In Montgomery, Alabama, Rosa Parks refuses to give up her seat on a public bus to a white man. She is arrested and jailed...A year-long bus boycott results in the U.S. Supreme Court invalidating segregation on Montgomery...

Free State Vs. Slave State

Before the Civil War, the United States was divided into Free States and Slave States. A free state was any state where slavery was illegal. A slave state was any state where slavery was allowed. The North wanted to make slavery illegal in every state! Southern states were not happy about that idea. They said that they needed slaves to work their land. Without them, Southerners would have no way of making money and their way of life would be ruined. The North and South could not agree on whether slavery should be legal or illegal. One reason the Civil War was fought was to settle the argument.

Activity

When the Civil War began there were 15 slave states and 19 free states. Color the slave states red and the free states blue. What pattern do you see?

Alabama- Slave State
Arkansas- Slave State
California-Free State
Connecticut-Free State
Delaware-Slave State
Florida-Slave State
Georgia-Slave State
Illinois-Free State
Indiana-Free State

Iowa-Free State
Kansas-Free State
Kentucky-Slave State
Louisiana-Slave State
Maine-Free State
Massachusetts-Free State
Maryland-Slave State
Michigan-Free State
Minnesota-Free State

Mississippi-Slave State
Missouri-Slave State
New Hampshire-Free State
New Jersey-Free State
New York-Free State
North Carolina-Slave State
Ohio-Free State
Oregon-Free State
Pennsylvania-Free State
Rhode Island-Free State
South Carolina-Slave State
Tennessee-Slave State
Texas-Slave State
Vermont-Free State
Virginia/West Virginia-Slave State
Wisconsin-Slave State

Civil War Forts

Some Revolutionary War forts were recycled for use during the Civil War!

A fort is a military structure built to protect soldiers, weapons, and ammunition during battle. Armies have built forts for thousands of years! One of the most famous forts during the Civil War was Fort Sumter. Construction on Fort Sumter began in 1827 and was still not complete by the beginning of the Civil War in 1860— 33 years later! Fort Sumter had five walls in the shape of a pentagon. These walls were 50 feet high, 5 feet wide, and 170 to 190 feet long! Over 70 thousand tons of granite had to be imported to build the fort. That's over 140 thousand pounds! Fort Sumter could house 650 men and 135 guns.

Fort Sumter is located in Charleston, South Carolina and can still be visited today, as can many other Civil War forts!

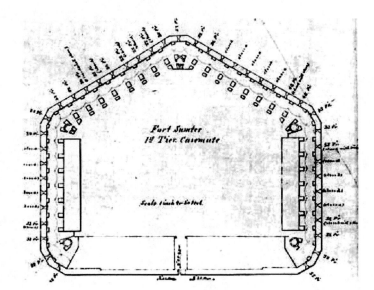

Fort Words:

abatis: fortification made from trees cut so that the branches face the enemy

breastworks: chest-high fortification made of dirt and wood

earthworks: fortifications made of earth

lunette: small, 2-3 sided structure that faced away from the enemy

parapet: low wall built to protect troops

rampart: steeply-sloped earthen ridge topped by a parapet

redan: breastworks shaped like a V facing the enemy

trench: long, narrow ditch

To Discuss:

• Why were forts built so sturdy?

• As Civil War era artillery improved, what might have been a threat to a fort?

• How did soldiers use the resources of the surrounding land to build fortifications?

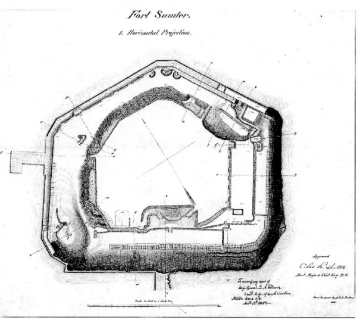

to owner…1858…Minnesota joins Union as free state…Illinois candidates Abraham Lincoln and Stephen Douglas debate issues of slavery; Douglas wins

demonstrate for equal rights in 100 cities, and over 3,600 are jailed…1963 …Dr. Martin Luther King, Jr., delivers his "I Have a Dream" speech…Gloria Richardson is the only black woman to lead a local civil rights group… Charlayne Hunter-Gault is

A War By Any Other Name...

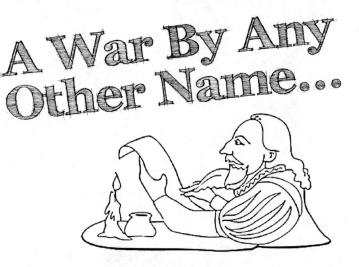

With our apologies to William Shakespeare, what IS in a name? Below you will find more than 20 different names used throughout history to refer to the Civil War.

FOR DISCUSSION

 Why would the Civil War have been called by so many different names?

Which names sound like Northern-created names; which like Southern?

 Which names would "push your buttons" if you were in the South? North?

How do names reflect our pride, bias, or other emotions and feelings?

20+ Names for Civil War

The War for Constitutional Liberty
The War for Southern Independence
The Second American Revolution
The War for States' Rights
Mr. Lincoln's War
The Southern Rebellion
The War for Southern Rights
The War of the Southern Planters
The War of the Rebellion
The Second War for Independence
The War to Suppress Yankee Arrogance
The Brothers' War
The War of Secession
The Great Rebellion
The War for Nationality
The War for Southern Nationality
The War Against Slavery
The Civil War Between the States
The War of the Sixties
The War Against Northern Aggression
The Yankee Invasion
The War for Separation
The War for Abolition
The War for the Union
The Confederate War
The War for Southern Freedom
The War of the North and South
The Lost Cause

What would you call the Civil War?

ection to Senate...1859...Oregon joins Union as free state...Abolitionist John Brown leads slave revolt; Brown is hanged...1860...Antislavery candidate

e first black woman to receive a degree from the University of Georgia...1964... Fannie Lou Hamer is a founder and vice chairperson of the Mississippi Freedom Democratic Party...1964...The Civil Rights Act prohibits discrimination in public

Red Badge of Courage

The Civil War greatly affected American literature. Many writers were interested in the war and used it as inspiration to write stories, poems, and novels. Several authors actually witnessed the war and had loved ones die because of the war. Some wrote love stories, some wrote about battles, and some wrote about why the Civil War had happened. These writings helped people better understand the Civil War.

The Red Badge of Courage by Stephen Crane
With an Introduction by Alfred Kazin

The Red Badge of Courage is one of the most famous novels about the Civil War. It is a fictional story written by Stephen Crane in 1895. Although Stephen Crane was born after the Civil War, his book depicts the sights, sounds, and senses of battle perfectly. *The Red Badge of Courage* tells the story of Civil War soldier Henry Fleming. Henry has just joined the Union army. After hearing that the army will soon march to battle, Henry becomes very afraid. He wonders if he will be brave during combat. Finally, Henry and his regiment go to battle. After the Union regiment defeats the Confederates, Henry takes a short nap. When he wakes up, he discovers that the enemy is attacking again! He runs away in terror, and is ashamed when he discovers that the Union has again won the battle. Henry feels like he can't go back to his regiment and eventually joins a group of wounded soldiers. He feels jealous of these men. He feels that their wounds are proof of their bravery. The wounded men keep asking Henry where he has been wounded. Henry is so ashamed that he is not wounded that he leaves the group of wounded soldiers. After wandering around the woods, he finds a battlefield and watches some of the fighting. When the Union army retreats, Henry tries to stop a soldier to ask what has happened. The soldier hits Henry in the head with a rifle. Another soldier leads Henry back to his regiment. Believing that Henry has been shot, the camp doctor cares for him. The next day, Henry and the regiment go back to battle. Henry fights bravely and courageously and his regiment wins the battle! Although, Henry feels guilty for abandoning his regiment, he learns that fear of war is normal. He puts the past behind him and looks forward to the upcoming battles.

Questions for Discussion

Although Henry Fleming was not a real Civil War soldier, he faces the same problems and fears of real soldiers. Read *The Red Badge of Courage* and discuss the novel. What do you think a Red Badge of Courage is? Were the men who got wounded the only soldiers that showed courage? Why was Henry so afraid of battle?

Activity

Write your own Civil War short story.

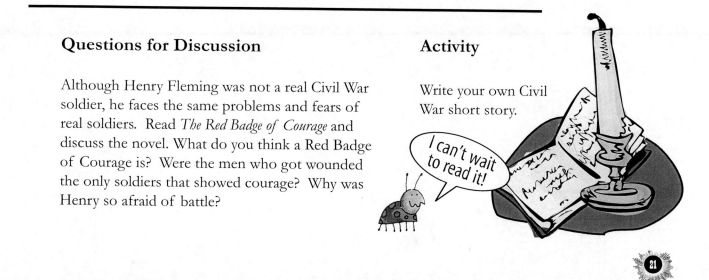

I can't wait to read it!

Abraham Lincoln elected president...South Carolina votes to secede from the Union...1861...Florida, Alabama, Georgia, Mississippi, and Louisiana secede from

facilities; in employment on the basis of sex, religion, nationality; and establishes the Equal Employment Opportunity Commission... Lawyer, Marion Wright Edelman establishes the NAACP's Legal Defense and Education Fund Office in Jackson,

The Signal Corps

The Signal Corps was very important to the Civil War. Since the war took place over such vast distances and during an era when there was hardly any such thing but sending mail, any communication tool that worked was used to get messages to the right people at the right time. A few of the methods used were:

SIGNALING

• Flags, torches, rockets, flares, or sometimes, signal guns were used.

• Tall towers or hilltops were used to help relay messages, but bad weather hindered efforts.

• Flags, for example, were waved in a certain pattern to indicate specific letters, numbers, or phrases.

• You had to think! A white flag against a snowy scene would not communicate well, would it?

• And, you had to have people watching for signals, day and night—and this made them easy targets for the enemy!

SECRET CODES

Since anyone might see the signals sent, secret codes were developed using ciphers. This might be a simple double wheel, where, for example: 2 waves of a white flag meant A. Unless you knew the code, you couldn't figure out what was being communicated. So those watching for signals also had to be able to interpret them quickly. Codes had to be changed constantly, as it was often easy for the enemy to figure out the meaning of the signals. This kept corpsmen busy as a school student learning a new language all the time.

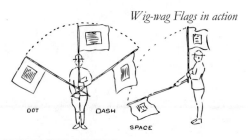

Wig-wag Flags in action

DOT   DASH   SPACE

TELEGRAPHS

During the war, the use of telegraphy became more common. Of course, a lot of wire had to be strung first, before telegraphs could be sent. Wires could easily be downed due to weather or enemy destruction. Often wire was strung, or re-strung, even in the midst of battle!

MILITARY BALLOONS

Since there were no spy satellites in the 1860s, the next best thing was to send a hot air balloon aloft and float it over enemy territory to "see what was going on." You might think these could be easily shot down, but artillery could just not fire that high. One balloon was made out of ladies' silk dresses! That must have surprised the "other side." But in a war, you have to use any resource available.

22

Jnion…Kansas joins Union as free state…Southern states form Confederate States of America…Jefferson Davis elected Confederate president…Richmond

Mississippi…1965…Septima Poinsette Clark leads an Southern Christian Leadership Conference group which registers about 7,000 black voters in Alabama…Voting Rights Act allows blacks to vote freely and unhindered…1966… Black Panther

Uniforms

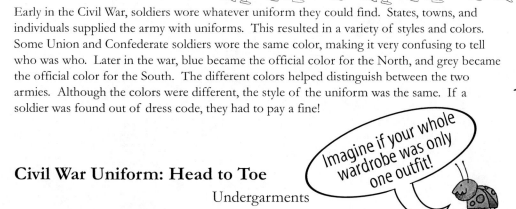

Early in the Civil War, soldiers wore whatever uniform they could find. States, towns, and individuals supplied the army with uniforms. This resulted in a variety of styles and colors. Some Union and Confederate soldiers wore the same color, making it very confusing to tell who was who. Later in the war, blue became the official color for the North, and grey became the official color for the South. The different colors helped distinguish between the two armies. Although the colors were different, the style of the uniform was the same. If a soldier was found out of dress code, they had to pay a fine!

Imagine if your whole wardrobe was only one outfit!

Civil War Uniform: Head to Toe

Undergarments

Drawers- All the men who enlisted in the army were issued one pair of drawers per year!

Shirt- Soldiers were given one shirt per year! Usually, they wouldn't last that long, and the soldier was forced to pay for a new one.

Socks- Each soldier was given only 1 pair of wool socks per year.

Trousers- Soldiers wore trousers or pants made of wool. They could be worn over socks or tucked into the socks. If it was hot outside, the soldiers would roll up their trousers.

Shoes- During the Civil War, most soldiers were known as foot soldiers. Instead of riding horses, these men had to walk everywhere. Sometimes they walked 30 or 40 miles a day. The soldiers' shoes would wear out quickly and new ones were hard to find. Sometimes soldiers had to march barefoot. When shoes became available, they were usually uncomfortable and did not fit. Soldiers wore boots but preferred shoes with broad bottoms and big, flat heels. Some soldiers wore an ankle-high shoe known as a "brogan."

Vest- Although, vests were popular, they were not given to the soldiers. The men who wore vests brought them from home.

Braces- Soldiers wore suspenders that were called "braces."

Like these?

Stock- A stock was a necktie worn for special occasions. A formal stock was made of polished cotton with a bow in front, and stiffened by a lining of hog bristles. A less formal stock was made of a square black neck cloth rolled up and tied in a bow.

Daily Garments

Sack Coat- Sack coats were durable, cheap, and easy to make. Soldiers had to keep at least the top button of the coat closed or they would pay a fine.

Forage Cap- Each soldier was given a forage cap. It was worn while a soldier was cleaning, cooking, or working in the camp. Some soldiers used it to hold collected food like berries and nuts. Although the forage cap was not "fashion forward," they were popular and comfortable to wear.

Virginia is named capital of the Confederate States of America...Texas secedes; joins Confederacy...South Carolina troops attack Federal Fort Sumter...Civil War

Party forms to establish black power in America...1967... President Lyndon B. Johnson appoints the first black U.S. Supreme Court Justice, Thurgood Marshall...1968...Dr. Martin Luther King, Jr., is assassinated in Memphis, Tennessee...New

Bon Appetit!

Knapsack- A knapsack was a waterproof backpack. Attached to the knapsack was a blanket rolled up with a "shelter half" (half of a tent). These two would be rolled up again in a rubber blanket that was used for a covering in the rain or a ground cloth.

Fry Pan and Spatula- Campgrounds had a "mess" tent where soldiers would go for meals. When soldiers were in the field or away from camp, they had to carry their own frying pan and spatula so they could cook their own meals.

Canteen- Canteens held a soldier's water. They were made of metal and covered with wool. Since the Union army did not have dishes, soldiers used half of an old canteen as a plate.

Haversack and Mucket- Haversacks were made to carry a soldier's food. Many soldiers used them to carry almost anything including newspapers, silverware, sewing kits, pocket knives, pipes, tobacco, combs for lice removal, and writing utensils. A "mucket" was a metal cup used as a mug, bucket, and cooking pot.

Cartridge Box- A cartridge box is a leather-covered tin container. It held cartridges for the musket. A "cartridge" is a measured amount of gunpowder and a bullet hand-wrapped in paper.

Cap Box- When a soldier pulled the trigger on his gun, a hammer hit a cap and caused the gun to fire. A cap box held caps and a pick that was used for cleaning the gun and caps. It was lined with wool to keep the caps from spilling out of the box.

Bayonet- A sword designed to fit on the end of a gun. Soldiers used this to fight the enemy when they were too close to shoot.

Musket- A type of rifle that fires "minie" balls. A minie ball was a new type of bullet that was cone-shaped instead of round and easier to load.

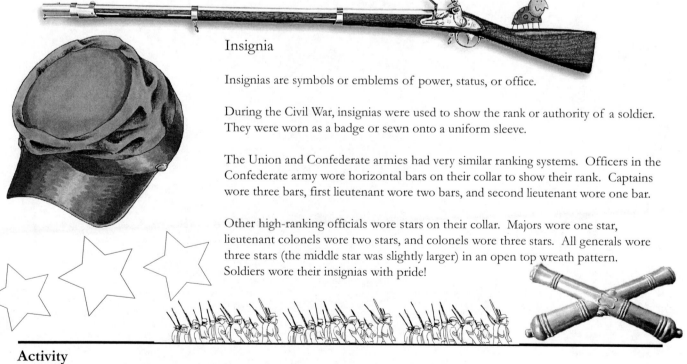

Insignia

Insignias are symbols or emblems of power, status, or office.

During the Civil War, insignias were used to show the rank or authority of a soldier. They were worn as a badge or sewn onto a uniform sleeve.

The Union and Confederate armies had very similar ranking systems. Officers in the Confederate army wore horizontal bars on their collar to show their rank. Captains wore three bars, first lieutenant wore two bars, and second lieutenant wore one bar.

Other high-ranking officials wore stars on their collar. Majors wore one star, lieutenant colonels wore two stars, and colonels wore three stars. All generals wore three stars (the middle star was slightly larger) in an open top wreath pattern. Soldiers wore their insignias with pride!

Activity

Create your own insignia. Draw an insignia that shows what ranking you are in the Civil War army. You can draw three bars and be captain or draw one star and be a major. You could even create your own ranking and draw an original insignia!

24

fficially begins...Federal Navy blockades Southern ports...Virginia, Arkansas, North Carolina, and Tennessee join Confederacy...Union defeated at Battle of

rk elects Shirley Chisholm as first African American U.S. Congresswoman...1969...Mary Moultrie leads a wage strike at the Medical College Hospital in South Carolina...1972...Political activist and intellectual, Angela Davis is acquitted of murder

Watch Night!

On January 1, slave-owners would examine their property and accounts. On this annual occasion, they would decide how their plantations could be more profitable, which slaves to keep and which slaves to sell. Slave families would gather together on Watch Night—December 31. It could easily be the last time they would all be together. On December 31, 1862, Watch Night had a very special meaning. Four million Southern slaves spent the night praying that President Lincoln's Emancipation Proclamation would go into effect the next day. Their prayers were answered and when the clock struck midnight on January 1, 1863, all the slaves were free. Since that night, New Year's Eve became known to them as Freedom's Eve. While the slaves were waiting for midnight to come, they invented a special recipe called Emancipation Proclamation Breakfast Cake.

Recipe for Emancipation Proclamation Breakfast Cake

Ingredients:
2 cups flour
3 teaspoons baking powder
½ teaspoon salt
¼ teaspoon cinnamon
½ cup sugar
1 large egg
½ cup milk
1-2 cups blueberries
¼ cup honey
Grated rind of one orange
Grated rind of one lemon

Cream sugar and butter, add egg and beat. Sift dry ingredients, add blueberries then add alternately with milk to the butter, egg and sugar mixture. Make dough stiff enough to handle. Pat out to ½-inch thickness on a floured bread board. Cut with a biscuit cutter and arrange in a greased pie pan in tilted fashion. Spread with honey and sprinkle with orange rind and lemon rind and bake for 15-20 minutes in a hot (400°) oven. Serve hot or cold.

Bull Run—first official battle of the Civil War...1862...1st ironclad ship battle between Monitor and Merrimac...2nd Battle of Bull Run ends in Union defeat

in a political trial in California... Equal Employment Opportunity Act passes...1974...The Coalition of Labor Union Women is formed...1978...U.S. Postal Service issues a Black Heritage postage stamp series...1983...Martin Luther King, Jr. Day is

Food Fit for a Soldier!

When a Civil War soldier was in camp, he usually ate pretty well, but the food was plain and not very exciting. Soldiers ate dried beef or bacon, beans, peas, bread, and coffee. When soldiers were on the move, they carried hardtack (dried biscuits), salt pork, coffee, and a little sugar and salt.

Hardtack and Johnny cakes were common foods for soldiers to eat because it was easy for them to make over a campfire and could be saved for days. The biscuits could be so stale, hard, and dry that soldiers called them "teeth-dullers." Sometimes the hardtack was moldy or infested with bugs, but the soldiers ate it anyway, soaked in their coffee, soup, or even cold water.

If you are making hardtack or Johnny cakes, you might want to enjoy yours with jam or syrup!

Union Hardtack

Ingredients:
2 cups of flour
½ - ¾ cup of water
1 tablespoon of shortening
6 pinches of salt

Preheat over to 400 degrees. Mix the ingredients together into a stiff batter, knead several times, and spread the dough out flat on a greased cookie sheet about ½ inch high. Bake for 30 minutes. Remove from oven, cut dough into 3-inch squares, and punch four rows of four holes in dough. Turn dough over, return to the oven and bake another 30 minutes. Turn oven off and leave the door closed. Leave the hardtack in the oven until cool. Remove and enjoy!

FRYING HARDTACK.

Confederate Johnny Cakes

I'll stick to dirt, thanks!

Do you want any?

Ingredients:
½ cup of cornmeal
¼ teaspoon of salt
2/3 cup boiling water
shortening for greasing the skillet

Mix the cornmeal and salt in a bowl. Pour the boiling water over the cornmeal and stir. Let the mixture stand for about five minutes. If the mixture is too thick to spread, add one to two tablespoons of water. Heat a lightly greased skillet or griddle. Pour the mixture into the skillet. You can cook the entire recipe at once or you can make small cakes. Cook at medium heat for about five minutes. Remove and enjoy!

..Battle of Antietam becomes bloodiest day of the Civil War...1st black regiment formed...1863...President Lincoln issues Emancipation Proclamation...Union

rst celebrated on January 20th as a federal holiday...1989...General Colin Powell chosen as first black chairman of Joint Chiefs of Staff, the nation's top military position...1991...Civil Rights Act limits affirmative action...1992...Mae Jemison

Animals of the Civil War

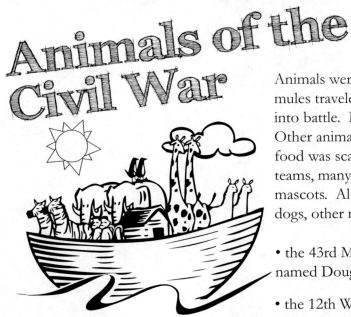

Animals were a very important part of the Civil War. Horses and mules traveled with the army to work. Horses carried soldiers into battle. Mules pulled supply wagons to different locations. Other animals like chickens and cows were used as food. When food was scarce, soldiers ate snakes and rats! Like today's sports teams, many regiments, infantries, and battalions had animal mascots. Although most mascots were dogs, other mascots included:

• the 43rd Mississippi Infantry's camel named Douglas;

• the 12th Wisconsin regiment and the 104th Pennsylvania Infantry's raccoons;

• a Minnesota regiment's bear;

• a pelican, eagle, badger, goat, squirrel, pig, cat, donkey, and goose!

Pick me!

Please don't pick him!

Often, the mascot would become a pet to the soldiers. Dogs went into battle with the men and on more than one occasion, a horse saved the life of its owner! Soldiers loved their animals so much that many statues and monuments were built in their honor.

Diaries and letters written by Civil War soldiers tell all about these pets. Several books including *Dogs of War* and *Horses of Gettysburg* recount the story of Civil War animal mascots. One of the most famous stories is about Sallie.

Activity

Research the different types of animals used as mascots during the Civil War. If you were in the army, what type of animal mascot would you have? Write a story about the mascot that you choose. What type of animal is it? What is its name? How was your mascot brave and heroic?

Sallie was a bull terrier that lived with the 11th Pennsylvania Infantry. She was a puppy when she first joined the army, and grew up as an army mascot. Sallie marched with the men everywhere, even into battle! During the Battle of Gettysburg, Sallie could be heard loudly barking at the Rebels. But when the soldiers were forced to retreat, Sallie got lost in the confusion. She walked for hours trying to find her friends. Tired and hungry, she finally gave up and went back to the battlefield. Sallie stood guard over the dead and wounded soldiers. Finally, a soldier found Sallie and returned her to her infantry where she served two more years. Today, visitors to the Gettysburg battlefield can see a statue of a soldier honoring the men of the 11th Pennsylvania Infantry. At the base of that statue is another monument—one of a brave little dog named Sallie!

War Department establishes Bureau of Colored Troops…Confederate General Thomas "Stonewall" Jackson killed… Grant conquers Vicksburg, Mississippi

becomes the first African American female U.S. astronaut…1993…Toni Morrison becomes first African American female to win a Pulitzer Prize in literature for her novel, Beloved…2000…President George W. Bush appoints African American

The Order of Command

With all those soldiers, and all that land, and all those battles, how were the Civil War's armies set up?

Fall in, men!

Fall where?

President		
General-in-Chief		
Major General ****	Army	
Major General ***	Corps	usually 2-4 divisions
Major General **	Division	3 brigades
Brigadier General *	Brigade	usually has 4-5 regiments and artillery complement
Colonel	Regiment	10 companies
Major	Battalion	5 companies
Captain	Company	(3 officers, 15 NCOs, 82 privates)

* = number of stars they had

FOR DISCUSSION

1. If President Lincoln had asked you, would you have served as the General-in-Chief? Why or why not?

2. Would you prefer to serve in the cavalry and ride a horse, or in the infantry and walk?

3. Would you like to have thousands of men under your command, hundreds, just a few, or no one?

4. What would the life of the lowly private have been like, compared to a general?

5. Which would be easier: having life and death responsibility for men, or just being an ordinary soldier?

ondoleezza Rice to serve as his U.S. National Security Advisor...2002...Tiger Woods becomes the youngest golfer (age 26!) to win 8 PGA major titles...African American tennis star Serena Williams wins the U.S. Open and Wimbledon

Medical Tools in the Civil War

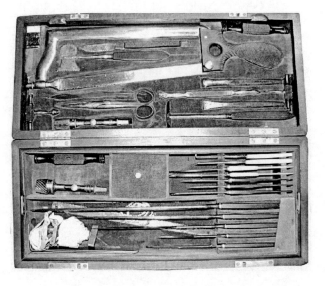

If the Civil War was all about battle and battle wounds, then it just figures that it was also about medical people, places, and things to help treat the soldiers. The doctors and nurses did the best they could with what they had, and with the far more limited medical knowledge available during that era. Think about it: germs were unknown, so doctors often stuck their hands in the guts of one soldier, and then in another, and another. Even something as ordinary as a stethoscope or a thermometer were rare and generally unavailable. Add to this poor nutrition, poor sanitation, contaminated water, awful weather, and more, and it was a recipe for, well, death.

Some wounded soldiers walked as far as thirty miles to get medical help, when no medical transportation was available.

Many soldiers were so young, they often came down with "childhood" diseases such as mumps, measles, and scarlet fever!

While relief agencies were few (it was a new idea), some one-woman relief organizations, like that of Clara Barton, were effective.
(She later formed the American Red Cross!)

While female nurses were not always popular or accepted by field doctors, most soon learned what a help they could be to soldiers.

The need for sterilization of medical equipment was unknown, leading to even more infection and death.

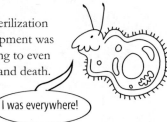

I was everywhere!

Some of the tools of the Civil War medical trade:

• Hospital tent

• A horse and wagon "rocker" ambulance jolted wounded soldiers

• A 36-stretcher hospital railway car

• A litter to cart wounded soldiers off the field

• A scary-looking metal device used as a tourniquet to stop bleeding

• A blunt probe—a metal stick to poke around inside you with!

• Amputating saws, knives; bone nippers (Ouch!)

• Very limited anesthetics (painkillers): often a swig of whiskey or a stick gripped between the teeth had to suffice

Gettysburg Address...Union forces gain control Tennessee...1864...Grant appointed commander of Union Army...General Sherman conquers Atlanta, Georgia

tournaments...Talk show host Oprah Winfrey receives the first Bob Hope Humanitarian Award at the 54th Annual Emmy Awards...Halle Berry becomes first African American to win an Academy Award for best actress...The Slavery Reparations

Civil War Casualties

Let's face it, it wasn't a pretty picture. But just how ugly was it? Let's let the numbers tell the tale!

Casualties of War

	Battle Deaths	Other Deaths	Non-Mortal Wounds	Total Casualties
Civil War (1861 - 1865)				
Union	140,414	224,097	281,851	646,392
Confederate	95,000	165,000	194,000	454,000

FOR DISCUSSION

• What is the definition of "casualty?"
• How did a lack of medical care, sanitation, no awareness of germs, and a lack of medicines contribute to Civil War casualty numbers?
• Are you surprised that "other deaths" outnumber actual battle deaths in the Civil War? What created these deaths?

Civil War Firsts

During a war, the world does not stop. Indeed, war often is a real instigator of imagination, creativity, ingenuity, and invention. Here are just a few "firsts" created during the Civil War years.

• 1st time a railroad was used to transport troops
• 1st Congressional Medal of Honor given twice, given to a woman as a doctor
• 1st "modern" war to use new technologies such as: telegraphy, photography, balloon observation, trenches, wire entanglements, repeating rifles, breech/paddding rifles

FOR DISCUSSION

• How does "necessity is the mother of invention" apply during wartimes?
• What things might have been used in the Civil War, if they had been invented sooner?
• What things have been invented in recent wars?
• In addition to war, what types of new and different events create invention and discovery?

TO RESEARCH

• When were anesthetics invented?
• When was the first blood transfusion?
• When were "germs" discovered?

...Maryland abolishes slavery...Nevada joins union as free state...Abraham Lincoln wins reelection as president...Sherman begins "March to the Sea" through

coordinating Committee, led by prominent African American lawyers and activists, announce plans to sue companies that profited from slavery... President George W. Bush awards comedian and actor Bill Cosby and baseball player Hank Aaron

The Civil War Numbers Tell the Tale!

But how many ladybugs were there?

Sometimes, in something as heated as war, we think our opinions count most, and perhaps they do.

But, no matter which side you were on or for, what "deductions" or "decisions" might you have made...just from the math?

1. Less than 10% of Southerners owned slaves.

2. At the start of the war, the North had 22 million people. The South had 12.5 million; but 3.5 million of those were slaves.

3. During the final year of the war, the Union Army had 1 million soldiers; the Confederate Army had 200,000 soldiers.

4. How would you feel about entering any new battle after calculating the average casualty rate from the Civil War's six bloodiest battles?:

Gettysburg 51,000   Chickamauga 28,000
Seven Days 27,500   Antietam 23,500
Wilderness 22,000   Chancellorsville 21,900

5. 67% of Civil War generals wore beards.

6. When war began, the North had 110,000 manufacturing plants versus 18,000 for the South

7. The North had more than 1 million workers in industry; the South had around 100,000.

8. The North produced 97% of the firearms for the war, 96% of railroads, and had 81% of the nation's banking deposits.

9. The North produced 5,000 rifles each day; the South, 300.

10. About 500,000 Africans were sold into slavery in the U.S. between 1619 and 1865.

11. The national debt was about $64 million in 1860 and almost $3 trillion in 1865.

12. The war cost the Union $2,500 per day in 1860, $4 million a day in 1865.

But I don't wanna!   Hand it over!

13. The Union spent $124 million on horses.

14. The value of all slaves in the South was estimated at $2 billion; the cost of the Confederate war was just about the same amount.

FOR DISCUSSION

• What can "numbers" tell us?

• When we "run the math" what can we learn?

• Are statistics important?

FOR RESEARCH

• What other Civil War statistics would you like to know?

• See how many more statistics you can collect, and explain what they mean.

31

Georgia...1865...Robert E. Lee appointed general-in-chief of all Confederate armies...Missouri abolishes slavery...Abraham Lincoln rejects Jefferson Davis's

the nation's highest civilian honor—the Presidential Medal of Freedom... 2005... Condoleezza Rice is appointed Secretary of State becoming the first African American woman to serve as Secretary of State...Hurricane Katrina hits southern coast

What Else Was Going on Besides the Civil War?

The world did not come to a stop just because America had engaged in a long, drawn-out civil war.

Here are a few things going on as the Civil War went on for four long years:

Yes it did!

Queen Victoria

All hail the Queen!

Are we amused? I think so!

1861:

• Kingdom of Italy created
• Queen Victoria's husband, Prince Albert, dies
• The steam-powered elevator was created
• Vaudeville is born
• The 1st transcontinental telegraph is operative

1862:

• The source of the Nile River is discovered
• There is a cotton shortage in England
• Concentrated fruit juice is invented

1863:

• Poland goes to war against Russia
• The 1st accident insurance company is opened
• Roller skating is invented
• The 1st paper dress pattern is created

1864:

• Thanksgiving is named a national holiday
• Pasteurization is invented
• The electromagnetic theory of light is developed
• The railroad sleeping car is invented

1865:

• The 1st woman is named as a professor of astronomy
• *Alice's Adventures in Wonderland* is published
• John Stetson opens a hat factory
• *War and Peace* is published

FOR DISCUSSION

• How can war drain a country's resources?

• How can war divert creative thought and action, as well as increase creative ideas and inventions?

• How might other nations affect a war in a country, even if it is far away?

• How can war affect the present in a country—for soldiers, families, towns, businesses, governments, etc.?

• How might war decimate land and create long term negative consequences?

• How does war, when there are many deaths of young men, affect the near and long term future?

• When a war is "over" how long does it take for things to "go back to normal" or do they?

• Can a war have positive consequences?

...eace proposals...13th Amendment to Constitution abolishes slavery...Confederates forced into full retreat...Confederate general Robert E. Lee surrenders to

f the United States...Ceremonial groundbreaking of the African Burial Ground in Manhattan takes place—the site will serve as memorial to 17th-18th century African slaves...Forbes magazine ranks Condoleezza Rice as the most powerful

11 Flags of the Confederacy

The Stars and Bars

As we know from reading news headlines, there is often still a lot of consternation and controversy over the Confederate flag. Actually there are many "Confederate flags." When the Confederacy was formed, it was logical for them to want to create their own flag, which they did. In 1861, a committee was formed to produce The Stars and Bars.

Boy, there sure are a lot!

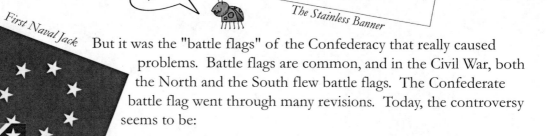

The Bloodstained Banner

The Bonnie Blue

The Stainless Banner

It seemed that the "Confederate flag" had complaints right from the start. Flags are powerful symbols and people are always very opinionated about a flag. One of the first concerns was that the original Confederate flag still looked too much like the U.S. flag, and so this was confusing. This resulted in several new designs for the flag.

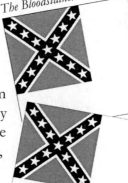

I'm seeing stars!

Second Naval Jack

First Naval Jack

Battle Flag "Southern Cross"

But it was the "battle flags" of the Confederacy that really caused problems. Battle flags are common, and in the Civil War, both the North and the South flew battle flags. The Confederate battle flag went through many revisions. Today, the controversy seems to be:

a. Is an historic battle flag ok to fly? After all, it is part of history. It represents the trials and tribulations and heroism of that army and soldiers.

b. Or is the Confederate battle flag an insult to African Americans, since it was flown during a war in which the Confederacy fought to keep slavery instead of it being abolished.

Flag Words to Know:
• Research and learn these flag terms: canton, field, hoist, fly, obverse, reverse, fimbration, standard
• Research and learn what these types of flags are: national, naval, battle, jack, ensign, pennant

Have students discuss:
• What is a "flag" but just a scrap of fabric in a certain design?
• Why is the flag such a powerful symbol?
• Do some people in some countries consider the U.S. flag an insult?
• Why do some people consider it wrong to fly or otherwise display the Confederate flag today?

Flag Trivia You May Not Know!
• The first flag to represent the Confederacy was the Bonnie Blue flag. This flag was never officially adopted.
• Early Confederate flags were hand-sewn by Southern women, often in patriotic "sewing circles."
• The final flag of the Confederacy only finally appeared just before the end of the war!

33

Union general Ulysses S. Grant at Appomattox Court House, Virginia...President Lincoln assassination by Southerner John Wilkes Booth...Vice President

woman in the world...2006...The Covenant becomes the first black book to reach number 1 on the New York Time's nonfiction paper back best seller list... 2007...Oprah Winfrey opens the Oprah Winfrey Leadership Academy for Girls in South

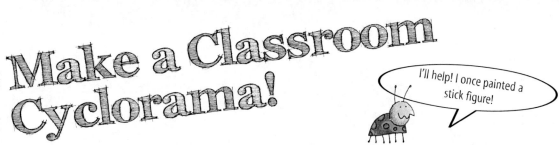

Make a Classroom Cyclorama!

I'll help! I once painted a stick figure!

A cyclorama is a giant 3-D painting of a historic event or famous place painted on the wall of circular room. Artifacts and figures sit on the floor and create what is called a diorama. Often, music of the time is played while a narrator tells a story. When a person stands in the middle of the room, he feels like he is part of the event! One famous Civil War cyclorama is the Atlanta Cyclorama. The Atlanta Cyclorama depicts the Battle of Atlanta fought on July 22, 1864. On that day, Confederate troops tried to save Atlanta from the Union armies that had surrounded the city. Although, they were successful at first, by nightfall General Sherman and the Union troops had won the battle. Over 12,000 soldiers were killed, wounded, or missing. The Atlanta Cyclorama is one of the largest oil paintings in the world! It is 42 feet tall, 358 feet in circumference, and covers 15,030 square feet. The painting alone weighs over 10,000 pounds! Although, the painting is large, the figures in the diorama are small. The tallest figure is only 3 feet and the shortest figure is 17 inches!

The Atlanta Cyclorama

Make Your Own Cyclorama!

Choose a wall of your classroom and cover it with poster paper or bulletin board paper. Choose a Civil War event that you would like to recreate. It could be a well-known battle (Gettysburg), a famous event (Surrender at Appomattox), or something that happened in your hometown! Have students research the event and draw it on the paper. Ask students to bring in "Civil War" artifacts (old boots, maps, pictures, war materials) to make the diorama. Hide a CD player in the scenery and play music from the Civil War era. Have a student recite a narration about your historical event and videotape that. When the project is complete, have other classes visit your cyclorama or have parents come visit and learn about the Civil War!

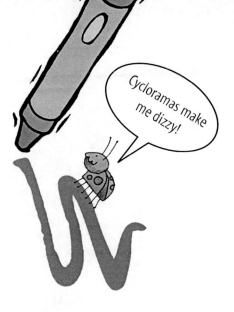

Cycloramas make me dizzy!

Andrew Johnson sworn into office...John Wilkes Booth shot and killed in Bowling Green, Virginia...President Johnson submits plan for Restoration of South

Africa... 2008... Barack Obama wins presidential election becoming first African American president-elect... 2009...Barack Obama is inaugurated as the first African American President ...Michelle Obama is the first African American First Lady...

Reconstruction

Reconstruction: the recovery and rebuilding period following the Civil War

Can you believe the war is finally over? The weight of the world has been lifted from my husband's shoulders. I can see it in his eyes. And we are going to Ford's Theatre to see a play tonight! A night of lighthearted fun—I cannot wait!— **Mary Todd Lincoln**

POP! What was that? Part of the play? Women are shrieking! A man has leaped onto the stage, yelled, and run off. The president slumps in his chair! I see blood! Can it be true?! Did someone just shoot our president?!—**usher**, Ford's Theatre

Stop that man!—**Major Henry Rathbone**

Everyone is sobbing. Our president died early this morning. May God have mercy on this country.—**newspaper reporter**

I accept this office of President of the United States with a heavy heart.—Vice President **Andrew Johnson**

Lincoln Shot!

He was in that barn and wouldn't come out. So we set it on fire! I saw my chance, and took it. I shot him. I shot and killed that John Wilkes Booth.—**Union soldier***

*The manhunt for John Wilkes Booth was the largest in history, involving 10,000 federal troops, detectives, and police.

Here are the latest statistics, Sir: 618,000 soldiers dead; probably 100,000 civilians killed too, Sir. That includes the North and South, Sir. And we know that disease killed twice as many as those who died in battle.— **Union soldier** *

*The Civil War death toll is more than the total killed in the American Revolution, War of 1812, Mexican War, Spanish-American War, World War I, World War II, Korean War, Vietnam, and Gulf War— all combined!

The Legend of *Taps*

In 1862, Union Army Captain Robert Ellicombe looked over the battle scene. He heard the groan of a wounded soldier. Although, he did not know if the soldier was a Union soldier or a Confederate soldier, the captain crawled through the battle amidst gunfire and carried the soldier to the medical tent. When he got back, he found that the soldier was a Confederate, but he was already dead. He recognized the face of the soldier and realized it was his own son. Because the son was a Rebel, he was not allowed to have a full military burial. Only one musician, a bugler, was allowed to play. The father asked the bugler to play a song that was found in the pocket of his son's uniform. The bugler played the song that became known as *Taps*.

This story is legend, not historically accurate

The True Story of *Taps*

General Daniel Butterfield was dissatisfied with the customary firing of three rifles at the end of military burials. He altered a French bugle call into what is now known as *Taps*. The song became very popular, and within months it was sounded by both the Union and Confederate armies.

This story is the true story of *Taps*. Not as fun and romantic as the Legend!

Everything is destroyed! Houses burned. Fields barren. Animals dead or dying—I can count their ribs. What has happened to our beautiful South?— **Confederate soldier**

When we said our vows years ago, I was just a child. Jefferson was 18 years my elder. My momma almost cried when I said I wanted to marry him. But we've had a happy life together. Full of struggles, I suppose, but happy. I never thought I'd be the First Lady of the Confederacy, not in a million years! But I stand by Jefferson in everything. Right now he's locked up, accused of treason since the great South lost this Civil War. But I'm staying right here outside his jail cell. I'll fight for his release until I feel him back in my arms again, no matter how long it takes.—**Varina Howell Davis***

*Jefferson Davis was released in 1867 thanks to his wife's unrelenting requests for his freedom.

My lifeless body hangs on the scaffold. Three guilty men wave in the wind beside me. They accused me of conspiring to kill Abraham Lincoln. I did no such thing!—ghost of **Mary Surratt**

If these old walls could talk, they would tell a history so fascinating and terrifying, no student would ever tire of learning about American events. I was built years ago, before any of these men were even born. My walls were erected for protection, but just look at them now. Spirits seem to haunt this sad and forlorn place, and will forever more.—**Fort Monroe**

...All Confederate states except Mississippi readmitted to Union...Six Confederate officers form anti-black society, Ku Klux Klan...1866...Congress passes Civil

Susan Rice is the first African American woman to become the United States' U.N. Ambassador... Eric Holder is the first African American Attorney General of the United States... 50-year-old pop icon Michael Jackson dies of cardiac arrest...Venus